MOVING UP WITH SCIENCE

HABITATS

Peter Riley

W

To my granddaughter, Holly Jane.

Franklin Watts
Published in Great Britain in 2016 by The Watts Publishing Group
Text copyright © Peter Riley 2015

Editor: Hayley Fairhead
Designer: Elaine Wilkinson

ISBN: 978 1 4451 3532 8
Dewey classification number: 570

Printed in China

Franklin Watts
An imprint of Hachette Children's Group
Part of The Watts Publishing Group
Carmelite House, 50 Victoria Embankment, London EC4Y 0DZ

An Hachette UK Company
www.hachette.co.uk
www.franklinwatts.co.uk

MIX
Paper from responsible sources
FSC® C104740
FSC
www.fsc.org

Photo acknowledgments: Ana Ando/Shutterstock: 5cl. Audrey Snider Bell/Shutterstock: 10cr. BMJ/Shutterstock: 14b. S Borisov/Shutterstock: 16b, 31t. Mark Bridger/Shutterstock: front cover c, 17c. Tony Campbell/Shutterstock: 15t. Rose Carson/Shutterstock: 10tr. Simon Colmer/Alamy: 21t. Alex Cotaru/Shutterstock: 8cr. Creative Nature R Zwerver/Shutterstock: 5clb, 30b. Ethan Daniels/Shutterstock: 1, 5t. Delpixel/Shutterstock: 18b. Jody Dingle/Shutterstock: 12t. dragon fang/Shutterstock: 12c. Dirk Erken/Shutterstock: 11cr. Irina Falkanfal/Shutterstock: 21b. Grigvovan/Shutterstock: 26b. Quang Ho/Shutterstock: 9bc. Miks Mihails Ignats/Shutterstock: 25b. irn-k/Shutterstock: 10cl. jack53/Shutterstock: front cover t. jps/Shutterstock: 10bl. Bernd Juergens/Shutterstock: 15bl. Juliet Photography/Shutterstock: 7b. Tan Kian Khoon/Shutterstock: 24t. Lebendkulturen.de/Shutterstock: 20b. Pim Leijen/Shutterstock: 19b. Tanya Lomakivska/Shutterstock: 8bl. Eleena Moiseeva/Shutterstock: 12b. Dmitry Naumov/Shutterstock: 7t. OJO Images/Alamy: 27t. Outdoorsman/Shutterstock: 11br. phodo/Shutterstock: 17t. Maryna Pleshkun/Shutterstock: 10tl. Alexander Potapov/Shutterstock: 9bcl. Sergey Ptakhotin/Shutterstock: 6b. Ksenia Ragozina/Shutterstock: 15cr. Valentina Razumova/Shutterstock: 9bl. RIRF Stock/Shutterstock: 23t. Panu Ruangian/Shutterstock: 11bc. Alexksey Stemmer/Shutterstock: 11cl. Maxim Tupikov/Shutterstock: 4b. Mark Velechovsky/Shutterstock: 10br. Vladaz/Shutterstock: 11t. Bertold Werkmann/Shutterstock: 27b. Richard Whitcombe/Shutterstock: 5b. Yur/Shutterstock: 9br. Zizar/Shutterstock: 19t.

Contents

Words in **bold** can be found in the glossary on pages 28–29.

What is a habitat?

A habitat is the home of a living thing. It is the place where a plant or an animal gets everything it needs to survive and **breed**. There are many different kinds of habitat. They can be as small as the space under a stone or as large as a forest.

Plant habitats

Plants need water, soil and light to make food. They need their habitat to have weather conditions that help them to make food so they can survive. For example, most plants need a habitat which is warm and light, with regular rainfall.

Rocks in a woodland stream provide mosses with a shady and damp habitat in which to grow.

Many fish live around a **coral reef** habitat because it is a good place to hide from predators and food can be found easily there.

Animal habitats

Animals need places to shelter from bad weather and to hide away from **predators**. They also need plenty of food in their habitat. **Herbivores** feed on plants, so they live in a habitat where plenty of plants grow. Animals that feed on other animals are called **carnivores**. Carnivores need to live in a habitat where other animals also live. **Omnivores** eat plants and animals, so they need to live in a habitat that has plenty of both.

producer of food

herbivore

Food chains

If a habitat can provide everything a plant or animal needs it will live, breed and make a **population** there. Each population of plants and animals in a habitat is called a **community**. Scientists link together plants, herbivores, carnivores and omnivores into **food chains**. A food chain shows how food is passed from one living thing to another in a habitat.

In this food chain a plant is eaten by a mouse. The mouse is then eaten by an owl.

carnivore

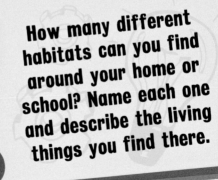

How many different habitats can you find around your home or school? Name each one and describe the living things you find there.

Plant groups

To make plants easier to **identify** in their habitat they are divided into four groups: mosses, ferns, conifers and flowering plants.

Mosses

Mosses are small green plants. They grow **stalks** with swollen tips, which let out **spores** into the air. When the spores settle on the ground they grow into new moss plants. Mosses often grow in damp, shady habitats, on stones or close to the soil.

Ferns

Ferns have huge feathery leaves called **fronds**. On the underside of the leaves are rows of green or brown swellings that make spores. The spores escape into the air, settle on the soil and grow into new plants. Ferns often grow in damp, shady habitats, such as woodlands.

These ferns and mosses can be found growing in a rocky habitat, sheltered from the Sun.

Conifers

Conifers are trees with long, needle-shaped leaves that snow can slide off easily. Most conifers have leaves all year round. These trees are called **evergreen** trees. They grow woody **cones**. Inside the cones, **seeds** are formed. In time the cones open and the seeds are blown away by the wind. Conifers are able to live in dry, cold habitats.

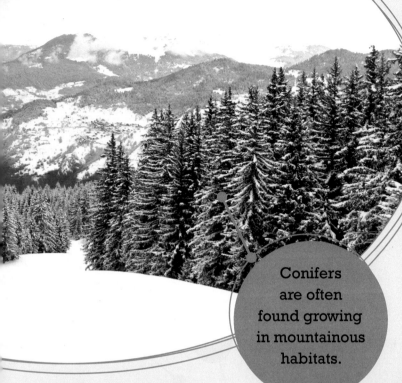

Conifers are often found growing in mountainous habitats.

Flowering plants

Flowering plants are the most common type of plant. Most flowering plants can only grow in a habitat with plenty of light, water and warmth. There are two kinds of flowering plant: non-woody and woody. Non-woody or **herbaceous** plants cannot grow in cold weather and die back into the soil in winter. Woody plants include trees and bushes. Most woody plants are **deciduous**. This means that they lose their leaves in the autumn and grow new ones in the spring.

A bright, warm day helps broadleaved trees and bluebell flowers grow in this woodland habitat.

Identifying living things

When scientists study living things in a habitat, they first need to identify them. One way of doing this is to use a **key**. It contains the different **features** of a group of living things. These are set out as a series of questions so that you can use the key to identify exactly which plant or animal you are looking at.

Identify plants in a habitat

You can make a key to identify plants by looking at and comparing their leaves. Look for plants on a patch of grass.

1.
Look for daisies, buttercups, clover and dandelions.

2.
Study each flower in turn and follow the stalk back to find a leaf attached to it.

Check the leaf shape

Look at the shape of the plant's leaf. You may find that some leaves are divided into three or more leafy parts. These parts are called **leaflets**. Now look at the leaf's edges. You may find that the edges are smooth or have little points. All these features can be used in a key to separate one plant from another.

Divide into groups

Divide the plants into those with leaflets and those without leaflets. Divide each of these groups into those with smooth edges and those with pointy edges. Arrange all this information as questions and connect them by lines to make a key.

Using the key

The key is read by starting at the top, reading a question, comparing it with the leaf and moving along the lines until the leaf matches the one described in the key. When they match, you can identify the plant.

Key for lawn plants

Is the leaf divided into leaflets?

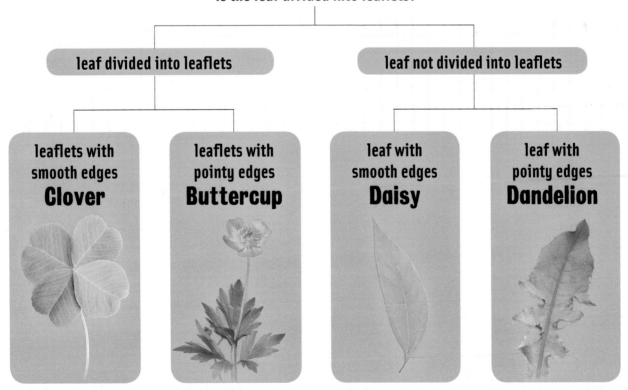

leaf divided into leaflets

leaf not divided into leaflets

leaflets with smooth edges
Clover

leaflets with pointy edges
Buttercup

leaf with smooth edges
Daisy

leaf with pointy edges
Dandelion

Animal groups

To make animals easier to identify in their habitat, they are divided into two big groups: invertebrates and vertebrates. Vertebrates are animals that have a skeleton of bone or cartilage; invertebrates are animals that do not.

Worms are animals with long thin bodies divided into **segments**. **Habitat:** soil.

Molluscs, such as slugs and snails, have soft bodies without segments. **Habitats include:** low woodland plants and spaces under stones.

Invertebrates

Insects have hard outer bodies and six legs. **Habitats include:** the ground, woodland plants, bushes and trees.

Spiders have eight legs. **Habitats include:** the ground, tall flowering plants, bushes and trees.

There are other invertebrate groups which contain woodlice, **centipedes** and **millipedes**. **Habitats include:** fallen leaves, rotting logs and spaces under stones.

Sub-groups

Each of these big groups is divided into smaller sub-groups according to the animals' other **characteristics**. Each animal characteristic helps it to live and grow in a particular type of habitat.

Fish live in water. They have **scales** and fins. **Habitats include**: seas, rivers, lakes and ponds.

Amphibians, such as newts and frogs, have a tadpole stage that lives in water and an adult stage that lives on land. They have smooth skin. **Habitats include:** ponds, low-growing plants near water, spaces under stones.

Vertebrates

Reptiles have scales and lay soft-shelled eggs on land. **Habitats include:** fields and woodlands.

Birds have feathers and wings. They lay hard-shelled eggs in nests. **Habitats include:** woodlands, trees and fields; beside ponds, lakes, rivers and seas.

Mammals have fur. They feed their young on milk. **Habitats include:** woodlands, fields, deserts, riverbanks and seas.

Habitats in spring

In many habitats there are four seasons in the year. These are spring, summer, autumn and winter. In spring the weather becomes warmer after the cold winter. This change affects the plants and animals living in the habitat.

Plants

In early spring some herbaceous plants, such as bluebells, start to grow new **shoots**. Their leaves spread out to catch the sunlight coming through the bare branches of deciduous trees. The plants use the sunlight to make food to grow their flowers. The flowers attract insects for **pollination**. The flower's pollen sticks to the insect, which moves it to another flower of the same kind so seeds and fruits can be made.

In early spring, this woodland is full of bare tree branches and snowdrop plants in flower.

An American robin sits on her nest to keep her eggs warm and safe. The eggs will hatch in 12 to 14 days.

Birds

During the spring, male birds sing or **display** to attract female birds. When a female joins a male they form a pair. They often build their nest in trees, far away from predators. The female lays a **clutch** of eggs and the pair often takes turns at keeping them warm until they hatch.

Insects

Insects can spend the winter as eggs, **pupa** or as **hibernating** adults, tucked behind loose bark, under fallen leaves or deep underground to keep warm. In the spring the eggs hatch and the **larvae**, such as caterpillars and grubs, begin to feed. Pupa break open and the adults climb out. Hibernating adult insects and those from the pupa then fly off to feed and breed.

Mammals

In winter some mammals, such as bats, hide away in a sheltered place and sleep. This is called hibernation and it keeps them safe from the cold winter weather. They wake up when the warm spring weather arrives and begin to feed and search for **mates**.

Describe the plants and animals that live and grow in a local habitat in the spring. How do they change through the season?

Habitats in summer

During the warm summer months, habitats are full of activity. More flowers grow and animals spend time feeding and looking after their young.

Plants

In late spring and early summer, the **buds** on deciduous trees swell up, then burst open. The leaves of the trees make it too shady for the spring flowering plants below them, such as snowdrops, and they die back. Through the summer more herbaceous plants grow their shoots and flowers.

During the warmth of the summer, all trees grow their leaves. In order to reach sunlight, herbaceous plants have to grow away from the shade of trees.

Mammals

During spring and summer, mammals lose their thick hair and grow a thinner coat to keep them cool in the warmer weather. Those mammals that have found a mate in the spring give birth and then rear their young.

The female deer **rears** her young fawn near long grass and trees to protect it from predators.

Insects

Many insects, such as flies and some butterflies, go through their whole **life cycle** from egg to larva, then pupa to adult, in the spring and summer.

pupa

Inside a pupa the caterpillar changes into an adult butterfly, which hatches out and flies away.

Birds

When the weather is warm enough, a bird's eggs hatch. A bird will feed its chicks until they can feed themselves. Some birds, such as robins, go on to lay another clutch of eggs and raise more chicks before the end of the summer.

A blackbird feeds its newly-hatched chicks.

Use the information on this page to draw a picture of the animal and plant life in a local habitat in summer. Include labels.

Habitats in autumn

In the autumn, plants and animals in a habitat get ready for cold weather. Animals store food. Herbaceous plant stems turn yellow and brown. The leaves of deciduous trees turn yellow, orange and red.

Plants

In autumn, many plants' fruits ripen. Fruits contain seeds that need to be spread so new plants can grow the following spring. Soft and watery fruits, like blackberries, are eaten by animals. Their seeds pass through the animals' bodies and come out whole in their **dung**. Some trees make nuts, which contain seeds. These are spread by birds and squirrels. The willow herb lives in an open, grassland habitat so its dry and hairy fruits can easily be blown away by the wind.

The leaves of deciduous trees change colour and fall from the trees.

Spreading spores

Fungi grow threads in the soil to feed off dead leaves and shoots. Then they grow the stalks and caps we call toadstools and mushrooms. Fungi reproduce by releasing tiny spores into the air. The wind spreads the spores, which form new threads in the soil of the woodland floor.

Fungi caps open like umbrellas and spread their tiny spores into the air.

Ready for winter

Mammals, such as squirrels, make stores of nuts in the autumn to use up through the winter. Male deer, called stags, grow **antlers**. They look for female hinds, so that the two can breed and have their young in the spring. Stags attract hinds by calling out to them and showing off their antlers. Other mammals, such as hedgehogs, eat as much food as possible to make them fat. The fat gives them energy while they hibernate during the winter.

Stags compete for a hind. This behaviour is called rutting.

Describe the plants and animals that live and grow in your area and the local habitat in autumn. How do they change through the season?

Habitats in winter

During winter, many plants die back. Lots of animals grow a thick coat or they hibernate to protect themselves from the cold. Some birds **migrate** to warmer habitats.

Plants

Bark protects trees and shrubs from cold winter weather. Herbaceous plants survive as seeds, roots, **bulbs** or underground stems in the soil. Deciduous trees lose all of their leaves to save water and energy during the winter.

Only evergreen plants, such as pines, holly and ivy keep their leaves in winter.

Birds

By winter young birds may live alone or gather in **flocks** with their parents and other birds. Some birds, such as warblers, fly away to warmer places to spend the winter. This seasonal movement from one place to another is called migration. Other birds, such as waxwings, migrate into the woods in winter where the trees provide protection from the cold.

Canada geese migrate from northern to southern America for the winter.

Insects

Most adult insects die at the end of autumn but some, such as the Red Admiral butterfly, hide away and hibernate as adults through the winter. Some insect eggs or pupa survive the winter in the soil, or in cracks in the bark of trees.

Some mammals, such as foxes, do not hibernate. They grow a thicker coat of fur to keep them warm.

Mammals

Many mammals eat plenty of food in autumn to help them survive the winter when food might be scarce. Bats use up this food as they hibernate. Other animals, such as squirrels, eat the nuts they stored in autumn through the winter. They forget about some stores and the seeds in the nuts grow into plants in the following spring.

List some of the ways animals prepare to survive the winter.

Water habitats

Water habitats are divided into saltwater habitats and **freshwater** habitats. Saltwater habitats include large oceans and smaller seas. Freshwater habitats include rivers, streams, lakes and ponds.

Saltwater

The largest water habitats are the oceans. They cover nearly three quarters of the Earth's surface. The sunlit surface of the oceans is home to the plants and animals that form **plankton**. Plankton becomes the food of other animals, such as fish and squid, which are then eaten themselves by animals, such as birds. On rocky shores, there are plants known as seaweed. Invertebrates, such as sea urchins, periwinkles and limpets, feed on seaweed.

Fish, shrimps and whales all feed on **microscopic** plankton like these.

Rivers and streams

The second-largest water habitats are freshwater rivers, streams, lakes and ponds. In the hills, river water moves quickly. It washes away mud and leaves the river bottom covered in pebbles. Caddisfly larvae and mayfly nymphs (young mayfly) may live under the pebbles. On flat plains near the sea, the river water flows more slowly and mud settles on the bottom. This is the habitat of worms and freshwater mussels, which burrow into the mud.

Mayflies lay their eggs on the surface of the water. The nymph hatches out and swims to the safety of the rocks and pebbles on the river bed.

Lakes and ponds

In lakes and ponds the water does not move, although the wind may blow waves across the water's surface. The open water contains plankton. The edges have water plants, such as reeds, and in shallow water there may be pondweed and water lilies. Snails and leeches live on the plants, while diving beetles and fish swim around them.

Small mammals, such as voles and otters, and wading birds feed on the fish in lakes and ponds.

? Why do you think you do not find worms and freshwater mussels in rivers in the hills?

Habitats across the world

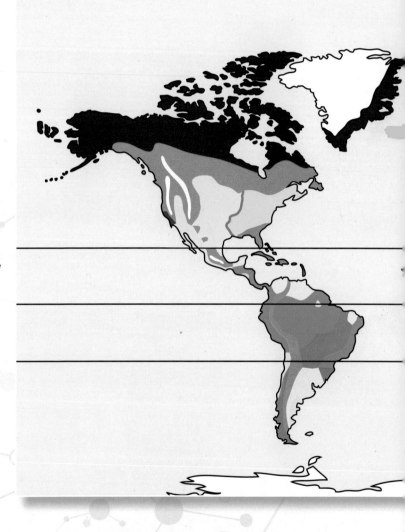

The weather varies across the world and this makes different land habitats, as shown on this map. Each habitat supports different food chains.

The polar regions are cold, with long, dark winters so few plants grow there.

A polar region food chain: plankton is eaten by fish, the fish are eaten by seals and the seals are eaten by polar bears.

The tundra is cool all year round but has a sunny summer, so some plants grow there.

A tundra food chain: reindeer eat the plants and wolves eat reindeer.

The coniferous forest has enough warmth and sunshine in summer for tall coniferous trees to grow.

A coniferous forest food chain: squirrels eat the seeds from the conifer's cones and great horned owls eat the squirrels.

The rainforest has hot, wet and sunny weather, which allows trees to grow to a large size.

A rainforest food chain: monkeys feed on fruits and eagles feed on the monkeys.

Bison eat grass in the grasslands of North America. They are large and have few predators, but they can be attacked by wolves and bears.

The temperate forest is made up of woodlands.

A temperate forest food chain: mice eat nuts and berries and owls eat the mice.

Tropical grasslands grow where there are seasons of hot; wet and hot; dry weather.

A tropical grassland food chain: zebras feed on grass and trees, hyenas eat the zebras.

Temperate grasslands grow where there are seasons of warm; wet and warm; dry weather.

A temperate grassland food chain: the saiga antelope eats grass. The antelope are eaten by wolves.

Deserts have very little rainfall and only a short season when plants can grow.

A desert food chain: locusts eat the plants and the desert fox eats the locusts.

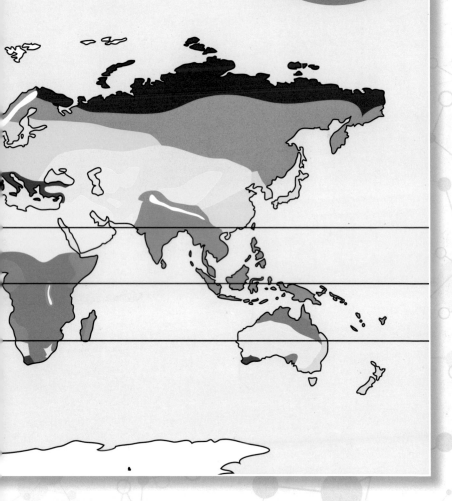

Scrubland is largely found around the Mediterranean Sea where the summers are hot and the winters are mild.

A scrubland food chain: insects eat plants, frogs eat the insects, snakes eat the frogs.

Draw a food chain for each of the major land habitats.

23

Humans and habitats

About 200,000 years ago, the first people on Earth lived by hunting animals and gathering berries, nuts and roots. They moved around in their habitat so they did not take too much food from any particular place or clear areas for buildings.

In Mongolia, some people still move from place to place through the year. They live in **temporary** homes called gers.

Farms and towns

About 10,000 years ago, people began clearing habitats to make farms. In time, towns were set up to **trade** crops and animals for other goods. More habitats were cleared to make room for town buildings and roads. Many plants and animals from these habitats died as they had nowhere to live, but some changed and adapted to their new habitat in the town. For example, foxes have been able to survive in towns by taking food from people's rubbish.

Habitats are still being cleared to make room for farms, towns, cities, roads, railways and airports.

Mining

Habitats are often cleared for mines, where coal and metal **ores** are dug out of the ground. Coal, oil and **gas** are burnt at power stations to make electricity. Metals are used to make many things including cars, furniture and cutlery.

Climate change

Every habitat has certain types of weather through the year. This yearly weather is called climate. Power stations, cars, lorries and aircraft burn **fuel**. This makes a gas called carbon dioxide. Too much carbon dioxide in the air makes the air hold onto more of the Sun's heat. Many scientists believe that the warmer air is causing **climate change** in all habitats.

Why didn't early people change their habitat?

How are habitats being changed today?

Saving habitats

All the plants and animals on the Earth live in habitats.
Each plant or animal can only survive in certain habitats.
If these habitats are destroyed, the plants and animals in
them have to learn to live in a new habitat or they will die.
To keep all the different kinds of animals and plants on the
Earth, habitats must be protected.

Use less fuel

We can all help habitats by burning less of the fuels that warm up
the air. We can use less electricity by switching off lights
and other electrical equipment when we are not using
them. We can walk more and use cars less. Cars burn
the fuels that make carbon dioxide. This warms the
air and creates fumes that lead to air **pollution**.

The money
spent by visitors
helps to fund the
work of nature
reserves.

Visit nature reserves

In many countries people
can pay to visit nature
reserves where mining
and chopping down trees
are not allowed. Hunting
animals is also banned.

Recycle

When materials, such as the metal in drinks cans, are recycled, they are changed and used again. This reduces the amount of habitats being destroyed for metal ore mining. Recycling also means less energy is used to make new things and there is less rubbish to find space for.

Clear away rubbish

Habitats are often damaged by litter. Animals can cut themselves on glass or choke on plastic. Rubbish covers plants and stops light reaching them so they eventually die. We can all help by clearing litter away from our parks and gardens, and by putting up posters to warn of the dangers of litter.

Clearing litter in your area is an easy way to help protect animals and plants.

Create new habitats

We can help to protect habitats by creating ponds with lots of water plants to attract animals. We can plant trees and bushes in our gardens and include nest boxes to attract birds and boxes to provide a roosting place for bats.

Add an insect hotel to your garden to provide insects with a safe habitat.

Glossary

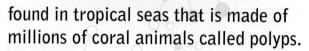

Antler a bony growth on a deer's head.

Bark the material that covers the trunk and branches of a tree or bush.

Breed to make more young plants and animals.

Bud a swelling on a stem in which a leaf or flower grows.

Bulb a short stem with food stored in swollen leaves. An onion is an example.

Carnivore an animal that only eats other animals.

Centipede an invertebrate with between 30 and 354 legs, one pair per body segment.

Characteristics a feature of a plant or animal that helps it survive in a habitat.

Climate change the change in the weather at a place over a number of years. When a habitat's climate changes the animals and plants there have to change and adapt to the new temperature and weather conditions or they will die.

Clutch the number of eggs laid and cared for at one time.

Community all the plants and animals living in a habitat.

Cone a woody case containing seeds made by conifers.

Coral reef a huge stony structure found in tropical seas that is made of millions of coral animals called polyps.

Deciduous a tree or bush which loses its leaves for part of the year.

Display when an animal or bird shows its feathers or performs a dance to attract a mate.

Dung animal droppings.

Evergreen a tree or bush which has leaves on its branches all through the year.

Features the parts of a plant or animal that can be used to identify it, such as the shape of the leaf or colour of its fur.

Flock a group of animals, such as sheep or any bird.

Food chain a line of living things linked together to show how food passes from one to the next.

Freshwater water that does not contain salt.

Fronds huge leaves that grow out of a fern from close to the ground.

Fuel a material that can provide energy, usually by burning it.

Fungi living things that have tiny threads that feed on dead plants and animals. They often grow stalks and caps to spread their spores.

Gas a material that has no fixed

shape or volume, which flows and can be squashed.

Herbaceous plants with shoots that die back after making fruits.

Herbivore an animal that only eats plants.

Hibernating when animals sleep through the winter.

Identify to find out the name of something, such as a plant or an animal.

Key a set of information or series of questions that can be used to identify a plant or animal.

Larvae the stage in an insect's life after the egg, such as a caterpillar that grows and changes into a pupa.

Leaflet a small leaf which forms part of a larger leaf.

Life cycle the stages in the life of a plant or animal.

Mate a bird or animal to make a pair to help in the process of breeding.

Microscopic an object so small it can only be seen using a scientific instrument called a microscope.

Migrate to move from one habitat to another because of a change in the seasons.

Millipede an invertebrate with between 36 and 750 legs, two pairs per body segment.

Omnivore an animal that eats both plants and animals.

Ore a rock containing metal, which is released when the rock is heated.

Plankton tiny plants and animals that live in the upper water of seas, oceans, lakes and ponds.

Pollination the movement of pollen from one flower to another flower of the same kind.

Pollution the presence of something harmful or poisonous.

Population a group of the same kind of animals or plants.

Predator an animal that feeds on another animal.

Pupa the stage in an insect's life when it lives in a case as it changes from a caterpillar to an adult.

Rear to look after young until they are old enough to look after themselves.

Scales small plates of tough material that protect the skin of fish and some reptiles.

Scrubland land with small bushes spaced out among herbaceous plants.

Seeds tiny capsules that contain a tiny plant and its food store.

Segment a part of a body. In worms the segments are all the same.

Shoot the part of a plant that grows above the soil. It includes the stem, leaves and flowers.

Spores very tiny cases that contain a part of a fungus, moss or fern, which can grow into a new fungus or plant.

Stalk a long thin support that holds up a flower or leaf.

Temporary lasting only a short time.

Trade exchanging goods for other goods or for money.

Answers to the activities and questions

Page 5 What is a habitat?

Activity: You might find small habitats, like under a stone or under a leaf; larger habitats, such as a bush or a wall; or very large habitats, like a wood or a field. The plants and animals you find in them will depend on where you live.

Page 13 Habitats in spring

Activity: You should look for plants in flower every week and note any changes. You can then measure the time in weeks that some plants are in flower.

You should also look for: insects visiting flowers; animals under stones; birds singing or visiting feeding stations; bats flying in the evening; the activity of squirrels; and keep a diary of what you see.

Page 15 Habitats in summer

Activity: The picture could feature trees and flowers, with deer and their young under the trees. A close-up of a twig with a pupa on it and butterfly emerging could be in the foreground. Other butterflies could be above the flowers. Parent birds feeding their young could be featured on the ground in front of the flowers.

Page 17 Habitats in autumn

Activity: You should look for plants in flower and those that are producing fruit. Do not eat any of the fruits. You should also look for the shoots of herbaceous plants dying away and colour changes in the leaves of deciduous trees. Note when each tree begins to shed its leaves. Look for animals collecting or eating nuts and berries.

Page 19 Habitats in winter

Activity: The young birds learn to feed themselves. Birds may gather into flocks. Insects may hibernate as adults or stay in eggs and pupa through the winter. Mammals grow thicker coats of hair. Some animals eat a lot of food before they hibernate and others make food stores to use later.

Page 21 Water habitats

Answer: Worms and freshwater mussels live in mud. In the hills, the river water flows so quickly it washes the mud away so worms and mussels have nowhere to live.

Page 23 Habitats across the world

Activity: Each food chain begins with a plant followed by a herbivore or omnivore, then a carnivore or omnivore.

Page 25 Humans and habitats

Answer: People did not take too much food from any one place at the same time so the plants and animals were not destroyed. Today, habitats are being destroyed to make way for farms, towns, cities, roads, railways, airports, mines for coal and metal ores. They are being harmed by changes in the climate.

Page 27 Saving habitats

Activity: Use a wooden box with a lip at the top to make your insect hotel. Roll up leaves and cardboard. With the help of an adult, cut a range of twigs or hollow reeds, such as bamboo, to the depth of your box. Using glue, stick the first twig or roll in one corner of the box and continue sticking more twigs and rolls until the box is full. Make sure the rolls aren't stuck togther too tightly. Hang the finished hotel close to flowering plants.

Index

About this book

Moving Up with Science is designed to help children develop the following skills:

Science enquiry skills: researching using secondary sources, all pages; grouping and classifying, pages 5, 8, 9; observing over time, pages 13, 17, 27.

Working scientifically skills: making careful observations, pages 5, 9, 8, 13, 17, 27; setting up simple practical enquiries, pages 5, 8, 13, 17, 27; using straightforward scientific evidence to answer questions, pages 5, 13, 17.

Critical thinking skills: knowledge, all pages; application, page 15; analysis, pages 23, 25; comprehension, page 21; evaluation, page 19.